Exploring South East Cornwall

Paul Lightfoot

First published in 2012 by
Alison Hodge, 2 Clarence Place, Penzance,
Cornwall TR18 2QA, UK
info@alison-hodge.co.uk
www.alisonhodgepublishers.co.uk

ISBN-13 978-0-906720-868
British Library Cataloguing-in-Publication Data
A catalogue record for this book is available from the British Library.

Designed and originated by
BDP – Book Development and Production,
Penzance, Cornwall

Printed in China

Title page: Moored boat and reflections, Polperro harbour

Acknowledgements
Thanks to the owners of Antony Woodland Gardens, Mount Edgcumbe House & Country Park and Cornish Orchards, and the Cornwall Wildlife Trust, for their kind permission to reproduce the photographs on pages 17, 21–3, 56 and 76; to the respective church authorities to reproduce photographs of church interiors on pages 13, 16, 61 and 86, and to Sue Lightfoot for preparing the index.

Contents

Introduction

The south-eastern part of Cornwall is sometimes thought of as a forgotten corner. It's as far as you can get, within the county, from the better-known holiday destinations along the northern coast and further to the west towards Land's End. And yet a little exploration reveals some of Cornwall's most beautiful and fascinating places, many of them all the better for being off the beaten track.

We will take a leisurely tour through the varied landscapes, natural and man-made, of towns, villages and countryside, the sinuous estuaries branching inland, and the sandy beaches and rocky coves along the coast. Where we can we will travel on footpaths and narrow lanes, which in the spring are lined with primroses, bluebells, red campions, ramsons and gorse.

We will make occasional diversions into churches and local history, sometimes following the path of earlier travellers and noting their observations. And all this in order to better understand the way that the modern countryside has evolved, and to better

Talland Bay: early morning colours in sky and sea

appreciate not only its beauty but also, and most important, how fragile it is in the face of the many pressures of modern life.

Much of the countryside is made up of rolling agricultural land, predominantly rich green pasture with pockets of deciduous woodland, in the spring interspersed with the deep shades of brown of ploughed fields and the bright yellow of oil-seed rape and cultivated daffodils; and in the late summer with the gold of ripe wheat and barley.

The farms are bordered by branches of the Tamar estuary to the north, sparkling and as green as the fields and trees that they reflect on a calm day when the tide is up, otherwise mud-banks patrolled by wading birds. To the south is the coastline, sometimes subdued, mellow and sunlit, sometimes rugged, spectacular and pounded by unremitting lines of breakers blown in by a southwesterly gale.

The old stannary town of Liskeard and the seaside town of Looe are the largest settlements. Torpoint with its naval training bases has always been closely linked with the city of Plymouth and its dockyard. Other villages and hamlets are small fishing and farming communities, often with colourful histories.

Bluebells in the woods above Sandplace, in the East Looe valley

Tourism in its many forms has come to dominate the local economy. There are hotels, homes and farms adapted as bed and breakfast enterprises and campsites throughout the area. Mount Edgcumbe and the villages of Kingsand and Cawsand attract regular streams of visitors from Plymouth, as well as from further afield. Looe and Polperro draw tourists from all over Britain, Europe and the rest of the world.

While the longstanding tradition of commercial fishing survives, local boatmen now derive much of their income from offering trips along the coast, catching sharks for sport and teaching sailing. Visitors are also attracted by the historic charm of the area's villages, by its natural beauty, its excellent walking opportunities and its wildlife. Of our area's four nature reserves, Looe Island with its colonies of seabirds and seals has a special appeal.

There is a wide variety of beaches, from Looe's popular and easily accessible foreshore bordered by the Banjo pier, to the three-mile stretch along the edge of Whitsand Bay and the coves of sand and shingle tucked into the cliffs of Port Nadler, Lansallos, Lantivet and Lantic Bay that are accessible only by boat or on foot. The coastal footpath from Looe to Polruan ranks among the best walks in the county.

The area includes ancient archaeological sites dating from the Bronze Age, and old mining landscapes. There are 20 churches, each with its own distinctive character and points of interest, as well as a multitude of Methodist chapels, many of them now converted into residences. Other historic buildings include military installations, castles and manor houses. One of the prettiest branch railway lines in England runs from Liskeard down the valley of the East Looe River to Looe.

We will start in St Germans, one of Cornwall's traditional entry points, from where we will travel south-east through Antony and on to the Rame peninsula; then westward along the coast, with diversions up and down the principal valleys along the way: at Seaton through the country park to Hessenford, the East Looe valley to Liskeard and the abandoned mines of Caradon, and the West Looe valley as far as St Pinnock and Herodsfoot.

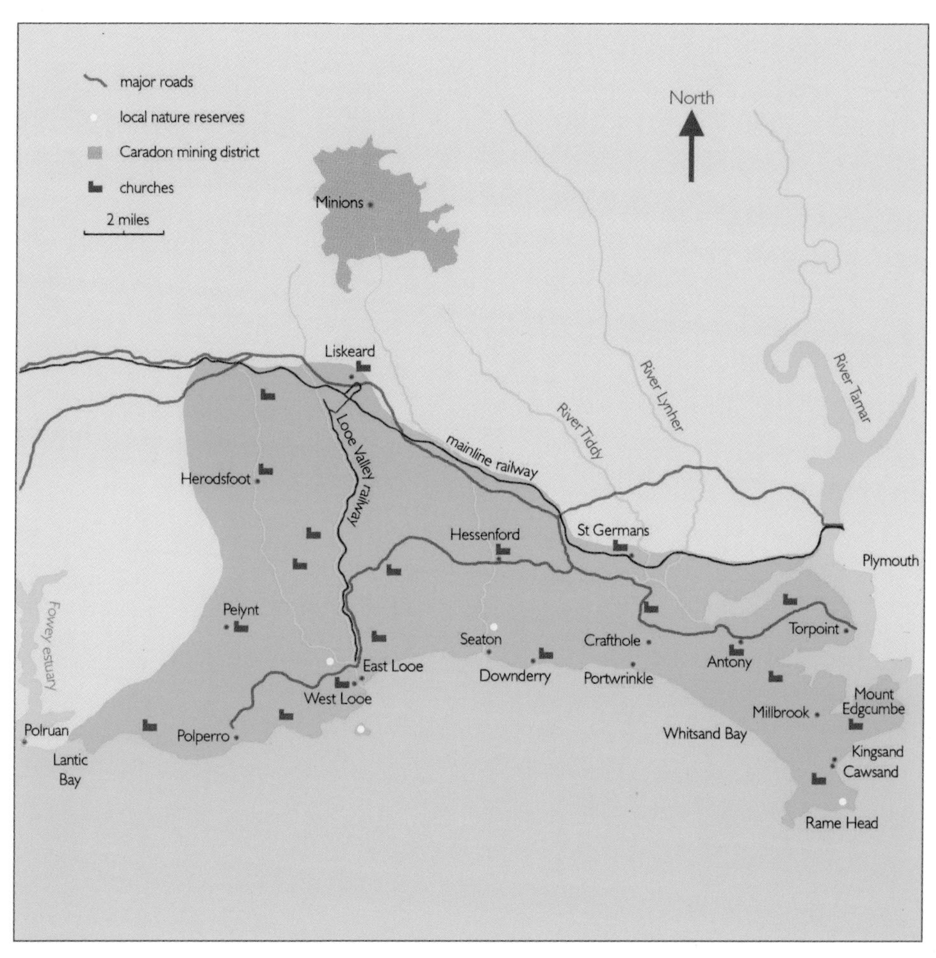

Map of South East Cornwall

St Germans and the Rame Peninsula

St Germans: The River Tiddy near Port Eliot (left); the church of St Germanus (right)

St Germans and Port Eliot

St Germans once had a far more prominent place in Cornish life than it does now. The village lies on a hillside above the River Tiddy, a branch of the Tamar estuary easily accessible by boat. For many centuries, before the coming of modern means of transport, it was the head of one of the main routes into the county. This is where Wilkie Collins began his *Rambles beyond Railways* in 1850.

It is also where St Germanus is thought to have arrived from France in the fifth century and established a base for his Westcountry missionizing. His original Saxon church, with an adjoining priory, became Cornwall's cathedral for 100 years prior to the Norman invasion.

The church was rebuilt in the twelfth century and, despite additions and modifications since then, it remains an imposing building both inside and out, and one of the best examples of Norman architecture in Cornwall. At its west end it has two towers, one of which has an octagonal top, and the other

Norman west door, church of St Germanus, St Germans

a square one; between them is a magnificent door adorned with a crafted metal cross and elaborate hinges, set in an array of seven concentric carved-stone arches. Every piece of stone around the doorway is original, the church guide tells us.

The vast interior of 'rounded arches and deep shadows' is 'the sort of place to plan an ecclesiastical murder,' according to Simon Jenkins in his book *England's Thousand Best Churches*. It is diminished by the absence of benches, which were removed late in the nineteenth century and replaced by the perhaps more practical but rather temporary-looking chairs.

Nevertheless, there is much to admire. The south tower has a peal of eight bells, of which the original six were installed in 1775.

The font, of Purbeck stone, dates from the thirteenth century, and somehow survived being thrown out and broken up, then reassembled and returned to its place in 1840. Fifty years later, a parishioner presented the elegant carved-stone pulpit and brass lectern. Near the choir stalls, there is some interesting carved wood, though much more has been lost during occasional renovations.

The church has two particularly outstanding features. The 9-m east window, installed in 1896, was designed by Edward Burne-Jones, a leading influence in the rejuvenation of stained glass art in the late nineteenth century and an associate of William Morris. Each of its ten lights beautifully presents a saintly figure in subtle shades of red, green and blue.

At the other end of the nave, in a dark corner where Simon Jenkins might have imagined nefarious deeds, is a startling monument in white marble to Edward Eliot who died in 1722. This is the work of Johannes Michel Rysbrack, an eighteenth-century Flemish sculptor who settled in London and whose work may be found in many of England's greatest buildings and public spaces.

Edward Eliot was descended from the family that acquired the priory, next to the church, in 1564. The building was in a poor state of repair until it was substantially rebuilt 200 years later, when it began to resemble the Port Eliot that we know today, though more changes have been made since then. It is still owned by the Eliots, who claim to have lived there longer than any other family has lived in a single house anywhere in England.

The Port Eliot estate extends for about a mile along the bank of the River Tiddy, and is probably best known as the site of an annual literary and arts festival that attracts nationally recognized performers. Recently, the house and gardens have been opened to the public for part of the year, while still a family home.

The house has a fascinating, quirky mix of artistic treasures and the memorabilia of the Eliot family, all cheerfully explained by knowledgeable guides. There is a collection of family portraits, many of them by the local artist Sir Joshua Reynolds, including the seventeenth-century parliamentarian John Eliot and the eighteenth-century military commander Charles Cornwallis. Surely the most impressive feature of the house is the beautifully and wittily executed mural painted over a period of 30 years in the 'round room' by Robert Lenkiewicz, which, bizarrely, includes seventeen self-portraits of the artist, among other recognizable people connected to Port Eliot in recent decades.

Church of St Germanus: St Mark, detail of the Burne-Jones window (left); part of the Eliot memorial (right)

Beyond its church and country house, the village of St Germans retains a quaint, picturesque character. Cottages of stone and slate line its main street, and there is a two-storey row of almshouses. Unusually for a village of this size, it has a mainline railway station that not only still functions but also offers accommodation in an old luggage van in a pretty siding beside the waiting room. Boats at the nearby St Germans Quay, overlooked by one of Isambard Kingdom Brunel's splendid viaducts, are a reminder that the village once served as a locally important port and supported a fishing industry.

Brunel's railway viaduct at St Germans Quay

Sheviock, Antony and St John

Before the railway came in 1859, most early travellers arriving in St Germans by boat would have continued on the road to Liskeard and places further west. We will do the opposite and take the road that meanders eastwards from Polbathic through Sheviock and Antony towards Torpoint.

St Mary's church at Sheviock is a delight, from its slender spire to the tranquil church-yard, the carved wood on the bench-ends and the magnificent east window that casts a soft light over the interior.

Beside the church, Georges Lane leads south towards the Lynher, eventually becoming an overgrown and muddy footpath down

The River Lynher from above Polbathic

to the edge of the river. From the end of the lane a ferry once crossed to Erth Quay on the northern side of the estuary. Now you might see a kayak paddle by, but nothing remains of any jetty that might have stood here.

In contrast, a mile or so downriver at Wacker Quay, a concrete platform and a few rotting wooden posts mark the end of what was once a military railway that served the nearby Scraesdon Fort. It is now a quiet little picnic area, ideal for watching gulls, egrets and other waders, and recently augmented by a footpath that follows the Lynher for a mile or so towards Antony House.

At the village of Antony a climb up a flight of granite steps to St James' church, above the Ring-o-Bells pub, is rewarded with a fine view beyond the square, two-stage tower and out over the Lynher estuary towards the moors to the north-east.

Clockwise from left: Carved bench ends, St Mary's, Sheviock; low tide near Sheviock on the Lynher River; remains of a jetty at Wacker Quay

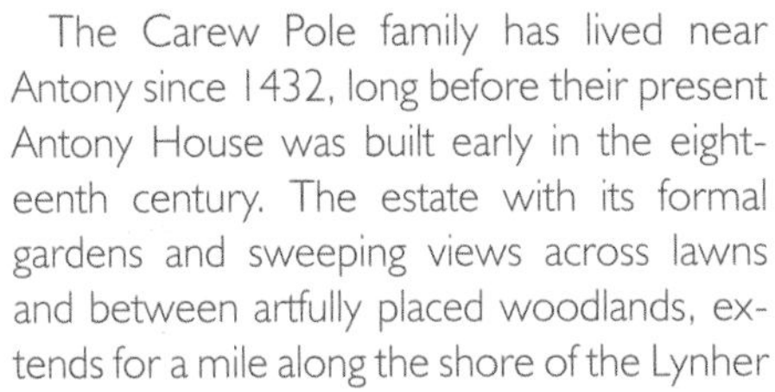

The Carew Pole family has lived near Antony since 1432, long before their present Antony House was built early in the eighteenth century. The estate with its formal gardens and sweeping views across lawns and between artfully placed woodlands, extends for a mile along the shore of the Lynher estuary, and inland to the Torpoint road. The family still lives here, but the house and part of the estate were given to the National Trust in 1961.

For many, the gardens are the estate's finest feature. They were initially landscaped by Humphry Repton 70 years after the house

Antony Woodland Garden (left); Antony House from the Woodland Garden (right)

was completed, but members of the family have added their own distinctive touches over the years. Now, we find magnificent yew hedges, a Japanese pond, a nationally recognized collection of 600 varieties of day lilies, modern sculptures in surprising places, and a fascination with cones: the roof of the original dovecot, the 9-m-high Yew Cone with an arbour cut into it, and a sleek, modern metallic fountain all share the same distinctive shape.

The Woodland Garden is the portion of the estate still owned by the family. It occupies a wide stretch around the shore of the estuary and offers extensive, beautiful walks through woods fringed with rhododendrons, azaleas, magnolias and camellias. On a rocky outcrop above Jupiter Point is a standing stone bearing an inscription from the *Rubáiyát of Omar Khayyám* – 'and still a garden by the water blows' – in memory of Sir John and Lady Cynthia Carew Pole, who directed recent developments in the grounds. Nearby, The Dell was used as the setting for the rabbit hole in the filming of *Alice in Wonderland* in 2008.

Inside, every room and corner of Antony House is filled with the fine furnishings and other possessions that the Carew Pole family has accumulated over the centuries. From the entrance hall to the bedrooms, the walls are lined with imposing portraits of leading members of the family whose exploits and relationships are set out in the guide, including two who were beheaded for their political beliefs in the turbulent times of the seventeenth century. On a table in the library is a copy of Richard Carew's *Survey of Cornwall* – the definitive description of the places and people of the county when it was written in 1602.

On the edge of the estate is the charming little church of St Mary Merrifield, built in 1866 from local stone with distinctive shades of brown and purple, and set within a pretty churchyard.

The town of Torpoint is a relatively modern creation. It has developed on the shore of the River Tamar since the mid-eighteenth century, initially under the control of the Carew Pole family, in response to the growth of the Devonport dockyard on the far side of the estuary. Lime kilns, quarries and quays were built, and ropewalks where lengths of hemp were laid out and spun into the hawsers, stays and running rigging required by the navy. But primarily Torpoint provided housing for sailors and dockyard workers. A regular ferry service has operated since 1791; in its modern form it claims to run the world's largest 'floating bridges' that haul themselves across the river on massive chains.

Tor House, near the centre of town, is Georgian; there is a Martello tower off Gravesend Point, and an active sailing community makes good use of the sheltered waters of the estuary. But for most, Torpoint is a place to pass through rather than explore.

The route from Torpoint to Millbrook and on to the tip of the peninsula passes through St John, a pretty village at the head of St John's Lake. This is an arm of the estuary where the saltmarsh attracts a wide variety of resident seabirds and waders – 'the greatest number

Autumn colours reflected in St John's Lake

of estuarine birds in Cornwall', according to the information board nearby. It is also an important resting area for winter migrants, and the European Commission has designated St John's Lake as a Special Protection Area for the conservation of wild birds.

Millbrook lies at the head of a sheltered tidal creek, a seemingly natural site for human settlement, and there are signs that people have lived here since as early as the Neolithic period. The earliest settlement, the earliest chapel and the mill that might have given the village its name were probably near the site of Insworke Manor, a little to the north-east of the centre of the modern village. Until 1865, Millbrook was part of Maker parish, and All Saints church was not completed until 1895.

Millbrook (left). The Edgcumbe Arms, Cremyll (right)

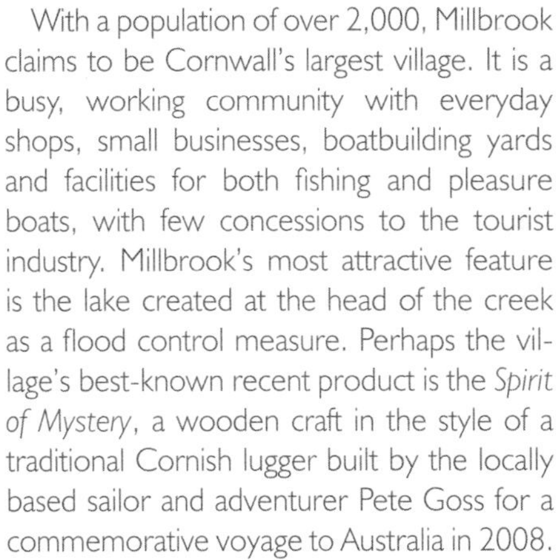

With a population of over 2,000, Millbrook claims to be Cornwall's largest village. It is a busy, working community with everyday shops, small businesses, boatbuilding yards and facilities for both fishing and pleasure boats, with few concessions to the tourist industry. Millbrook's most attractive feature is the lake created at the head of the creek as a flood control measure. Perhaps the village's best-known recent product is the *Spirit of Mystery*, a wooden craft in the style of a traditional Cornish lugger built by the locally based sailor and adventurer Pete Goss for a commemorative voyage to Australia in 2008.

The road around the lake passes an old lime kiln and late-Georgian houses, often with pretty gardens, through Anderton and along the shore to Cremyll and an entrance to Mount Edgcumbe House and Country Park.

We have now entered one of the twelve parts of Cornwall's Area of Outstanding Natural Beauty (AONB). The Rame section includes the coast from Cremyll to Polhawn Cove, to the west of Rame Head. AONBs are considered to be the country's 'most special landscapes'. They are defined and declared in order to provide a legal basis for protection against all development that does not 'enhance the character of the AONB'; in practice, Cornwall Council has much discretion in deciding how protective it wants to be.

Like St Germans, Cremyll was once an important entry point into Cornwall, at the head of a route that passed through Crafthole on the way to Liskeard. Ferries have crossed between here and Stonehouse in Plymouth for many centuries, and there is now an all-season, half-hourly service for passengers and cyclists. Hikers might want to fortify themselves in the Edgcumbe Arms before setting off around the coast, or recover there afterwards while watching the never-ending traffic of naval ships, tugs and sailing boats passing between the Tamar and Plymouth Sound.

Mount Edgcumbe

Mount Edgcumbe is the third of the great estates in our area. The Edgcumbe family built the original house in the sixteenth century as an escape from their main home at Cotehele, a few miles up the Tamar Valley. It was an early example of a house designed and built mainly for its views rather than for its defensive position. The family moved here 100 years later, although connections between the two houses continued for many years afterwards.

In the eighteenth century, Mount Edgcumbe house was restyled; the Earl's Garden was laid out on its eastern side, and the remainder of the estate became one of the first landscaped parks in England. Among other visitors, Captain James Cook and Charles Darwin honed their botanical observation and recording skills here.

Part of the National Camellia Collection in the grounds of Mount Edgcumbe

The house was almost destroyed by bombs in the Second World War, but a sensitive restoration was completed in 1964. It was rebuilt on a more manageable scale within part of the original structure, retaining its octagonal corner towers and long, elegant window frames. The external red sandstone

Mount Edgcumbe House

and granite walls were rebuilt without the grey render of the pre-war building. Cornwall Council and Plymouth City Council now jointly own the house and its 350-ha estate.

The beautiful neo-Georgian interior is furnished with surviving family possessions. There are portraits by many artists including Joshua Reynolds, whom we met in Port Eliot, and seascapes by the seventeenth-century Dutch artist Willem van de Velde. Among many remarkable features are three sixteenth-century Flemish tapestries hanging in the dining room. Recently restored, as well as being striking works of art, they depict instructive medieval pastoral scenes.

As at Port Eliot and Antony House, the grounds of Mount Edgcumbe include formal gardens, sweeping lawns and areas of less-manicured woodland with daffodils and other spring flowers. The Earl's Garden, next to the house, includes flowerbeds lined with ancient and unusual trees and classical stat-

The Italian formal garden, Mount Edgcumbe

ues. On the slopes above the house leading to the Amphitheatre, the footpaths are lined with camellias – an impressive sight in the early-spring flowering season. These are part of the National Camellia Collection that has been built up since 1976 and now includes about 1,000 varieties.

On the lower slopes, behind the old Garden Battery that overlooks the shore, are French, Italian and English gardens, and the recently added areas devoted to American and New Zealand plants, all enclosed by a 9-m hedge which is a remarkable feature in itself. The Italian garden with its fountain and statues lies next to the Orangery, built in the eighteenth century as a greenhouse for growing orange trees brought from Turkey, and now a restaurant.

The Earl's Drive leads from the house on a level, curved path parallel to the coast, with magnificent views over Plymouth Sound and coves that have sheltered ships for 1,000 years. Along the way, the Drive passes the deer park; historic, ornamental seats where walkers may pause and look out over Drake's Island towards the city and the Devon shore to the east; and the appropriately named Folly, a stone structure that was designed and built as a ruin in the eighteenth century.

Before leaving the estate, it is worth taking a detour inland to Maker church. The original building probably dated from very early in the Christian era and was located close to the sixth-century Holy Well of St Julian. The church was rebuilt about 1500, 'restored' in the nineteenth century, and, according to John Betjeman in his *Cornwall: A Shell Guide*, 1964, 'much Victorian damage has been undone by some sensitive modern furnishings.' Its 20-m tower has traditionally served as an aid to navigation for ships approaching Plymouth Sound from the south and west. Memorials to the Edgcumbe family are prominent features inside the church.

The best-known annual event associated with Mount Edgcumbe is its classic car show, arranged in August by the charity Friends of Mount Edgcumbe Country Park. Volunteer members of the Friends also undertake projects to improve the estate and its facilities, and arrange occasional nature walks and musical and educational events.

Kingsand, Cawsand and Rame Head

The coastal footpath passes around the edge of the Mount Edgcumbe estate, past Fort Picklecombe – originally built to defend Plymouth Sound, but now converted into private apartments – and on to Cawsand Bay and the twin villages of Kingsand and Cawsand. Each of them borders a sandy cove, separated by an elevated rocky promontory crossed by a narrow lane. Tony Carne's book, *Cornwall's Forgotten Corner* provides a detailed account of both villages and the surrounding area.

Kingsand is thought to be named for Henry VII, who is believed to have come ashore here in 1484. The clock tower on the edge of the beach was built in 1911 to commemorate the coronation of King George V. Cawsand has the excellent seventeenth-century Cross Keys pub, beside a square with a stone monument erected by the Countess of Mount Edgcumbe in 1871. Until 1841 the villages lay in different counties, Kingsand in Devon and Cawsand in Cornwall, with the boundary running between them.

The two villages share a similar history, originally dependent on fishing, but restrict-

The rocky foreshore and beach at Kingsand

ed by their exposure to raiding parties from Holland, Spain, France and the Mediterranean. As for all the villages and towns along Cornwall's southern coast, fishermen risked being captured by 'Turks' (Barbary Corsairs of the North African coast) and sold as slaves.

The narrow streets and hidden footpaths, and proximity to Plymouth, made Kingsand and Cawsand well suited to smuggling, which reached a peak in the late eighteenth century. The villages were among Cornwall's largest centres of boats and men involved in illegal trade, and many a cunning plan was devised for getting liquor across the Sound and into the city. Security improved when the navy adopted Cawsand Bay as one of its main anchorages in the late eighteenth and early nineteenth centuries; meanwhile, by 1820

Cawsand: The beach (left); Cross Keys (above)

the coastguard was well established along the coast, and officers were based in Cawsand. The villages became safer, but smuggling was riskier and had practically died out by 1850.

Both the modern villages have managed to remain picturesque, while escaping the worst of the commercialization that often accompanies the tourism industry; there is still some truth in John Betjeman's description of them as unspoiled versions of Polperro. The houses are pretty, often oddly shaped, pastel coloured with well-kept flower gardens, packed together lining the shore and narrow streets. Both villages are overlooked by wooded hills, and a massive old, grey limestone gun battery that is now divided into apartments. In spring and summer small boats are drawn up on the beaches or moored offshore, and a passenger ferry links Cawsand's beach with the Barbican in Plymouth.

From Cawsand, the coastal footpath continues to Penlee Point, the south-east extremity of the Rame peninsula, past woods that were originally planted for pheasant shooting, and above Pier Cove and other small, secluded inlets once used by smugglers to store their barrels and caskets until they could be safely sold on.

Rame Head

Above the footpath, and at the end of a narrow military road from Rame, are the remains of the Penlee Battery. It was built in 1899 to defend Plymouth; but the huge guns originally installed were so big that they damaged their mountings when fired, and had to be dismantled. The site was brought back into service for the world wars, but eventually abandoned and cleared.

The Battery is now a nature reserve, with little sign of its military past. Managed by the Cornwall Wildlife Trust, the reserve includes areas of woodland broken by open grassland, and is noted for its flowering plants, including the bee orchid, as well as adders, foxes, stoats, weasels and many species of birds and butterflies. The invasive montbretia is also widespread, as it is along much of the coast in summer. Perhaps because of its remote location on the edge of the English Channel, bird watchers regularly report unusual sightings both within the reserve and

Large white butterfly on knapweed, Penlee Battery Nature Reserve (left). Lich-gate, Rame church (right)

in the surrounding countryside. Colonies of bats occupy derelict underground buildings. The history of the site and symbols of its wildlife are carved into a five-ton granite boulder brought from Bodmin Moor, now lying next to one of the pathways near the entrance from the car-park.

The footpath follows the curve of the coast above steeply sloping, bracken-covered cliffs towards the distinctive shape of Rame Head, guarded by the remains of an Iron Age fort and with the fourteenth-century St Michael's chapel perched on its peak. Rame Head is surely the most unmistakable landmark along this stretch of coast, and is visible from many miles to the west. Not surprisingly, it has served as a lookout point from very early times: among many historically important events, watchmen stationed here would have seen the intimidating sight of the Spanish Armada passing by a few miles offshore in 1588. A permanent modern lookout station remains a reassuring presence.

Inland, Rame church was dedicated to St Germanus in 1259, though on the site of an older building. Like St Mary's at Sheviock it has a spire, another distinctive local landmark, and the churchyard includes a section for unknown victims of wrecks found along the coast nearby. Some fifteenth-century wood carving fortunately survived Victorian restoration work; the attractive lich-gate is a nineteenth-century addition. The church has no mains electricity, and is well known for its candlelit services. A measure of the church's popularity is the speed with which it raised funds for major repairs to the roof in 2010.

Whitsand Bay to Looe

Whitsand Bay, looking west along the beach at low tide

On the western side of Rame Head, we have wonderful views of the grand sweep of Whitsand Bay stretching to Looe in the distance, and, on a clear day, as far as Dodman Point and the Lizard. The Bay is at its best at low tide; with a south-westerly breeze blowing in, surf carries white foam over the sand far below. In summer, people might be visible as dots on the beaches; but Whitsand is never crowded, and in winter is usually deserted.

There were cellars at Long Cove and Crane Cove under the rocky cliffs at the eastern end of the bay, where Cawsand fishermen stored their catches. Polhawn Fort was built into the cliffs in the nineteenth century as yet another defensive structure that never saw military action; it is now privately owned and marketed as a place for weddings.

As at Penlee Battery, Rame Head and the cliffs and beaches of Whitsand Bay are almost always rewarding sites for bird watchers. Several species of seabirds and raptors are commonly observed, together with migrants passing through in spring and autumn. Typically, ravens, sparrowhawks, buzzards, kestrels and peregrines soar above, while in summer fulmars and Manx shearwaters may be seen cruising offshore.

Beyond Polhawn Cove we leave the AONB, and its protection of the landscape is plainly missed. Soon after 1930, when the military road opened to the public, some of Plymouth's aspiring residents built bungalows on the cliffs for weekends and holidays. From here the views over Whitsand Bay and out to sea are spectacular. Construction standards have improved over the years, so not surprisingly modern bungalows can fetch aston-

Daffodils near Tregantle, Whitsand Bay

ishing prices when they come on to the market. Even so, this largely unplanned, inelegant development has done nothing to enhance what would otherwise be among the finest coastal landscapes in southern Cornwall.

Long before the huts appeared, these views were put to good use. Fish spotters, or huers, from the competing villages of Cawsand, Portwrinkle and Looe would hide on the cliffs to guide their respective fleets of boats towards shoals of pilchards that were difficult to see from lower down.

Above Wiggle Cliff, walkers heading along the coast have a choice. The coastal footpath follows the top of the sloping cliffs all the way to Downderry and beyond, with a diversion inland and along the road around Tregantle Fort. This route passes close to what little remains of the Whitesand [sic] Bay Battery, built in the 1890s with guns set at a high angle so that shells would better penetrate the decks of raiding ships.

Alternatively, when the tide is down, and with an eye on the times of low and high water, you can walk along the beach as far as Portwrinkle, though with the risk of getting wet feet at Sharrow Point, below Freathy. The several tracks that zigzag down to the beach were originally for farmers to bring up sand and seaweed to fertilize their fields. Near Freathy there was once a tea-room and other entertainment for the tourists of 100 years ago; now there are the remains of fish cellars and the Sharrow Grotto, a large cave dug out in 1784 by an eccentric naval lieutenant who believed the exercise would cure his gout.

The massive limestone fort at Tregantle was built in 1865 as part of a ring of defensive structures around the city and dockyard at Plymouth. It was designed as a base for 35 big naval guns, to be managed by 1,000 soldiers. In practice this was another 'Palmerston Folly' that was never used as intended. The fort was already obsolete in the nineteenth century, and the full set of guns was never deployed. It served as a base for American troops in 1944, and more recently as a defence and training base for the army and navy, as part of the navy's Fleet Electronic Warfare Support Group, and as a site for shooting practice; hence the large 'danger area' that the Ordnance Survey map shows on the cliffs, beach and sea below.

A little inland from the coast lies the village of Crafthole, once a resting place for travellers at a junction on the old route into Cornwall from Cremyll, with roads leading further west along the coast or north towards St Germans and on to Liskeard. It was already

Figures on Finnygook beach, Portwrinkle

a borough in the early fourteenth century, although traffic declined when the turnpike from Antony through Sheviock was completed in 1820. An ancient stone cross beside the road probably marks an old route for pilgrims who travelled through the county.

The modern village is pretty where the road narrows to pass between old whitewashed cottages. Remarkably for such a small place, two inns continue to serve travellers, both with long histories from the fourteenth or fifteenth century. One of them, the Finnygook, is said to be named after an old smuggler called Silas Finny, whose 'gook' still haunts the neighbouring fields and lanes.

Finnygook Lane leads down to the coast, past a golf course and a stone dovecot and on to the fishing village of Portwrinkle where

Portwrinkle: The golf course (top); Whitsand Bay Hotel (above left); coastguard cottages (above right)

The harbour at Portwrinkle

Silas landed his catch, legal and illegal. Portwrinkle is thought to have grown in the seventeenth century in response to the demand for pilchards from places as far away as Spain and Italy, but the fishermen soon learned that they could profit more from bringing in brandy. As elsewhere, smuggling declined rapidly soon after the coastguard arrived in the 1820s; a team of officers was based here, and two rows of their cottages are still recognizable above the beach.

For 100 years the village has been dominated by Whitsand Bay Hotel, originally a Victorian manor house owned by Lord Graves, which also serves as the clubhouse of the golf course that extends back up the hill towards Crafthole. Few courses in England can equal its wonderful views over the bay.

Portwrinkle harbour is unlike any other, a simple little basin of sand and shingle when the tide is low, enclosed by stone quays. In summer one or two small boats may be afloat, with a few more stored on the slipway above, and another bobbing around offshore, hauling in a modest catch to raise a few pounds or share with neighbours. The sandy cove to the east is called – what else? – Finnygook beach. Between it and the harbour, the falling tide reveals a series of parallel, south-east-marching columns of jagged rocks – a boatman's nightmare but a haven for marine wildlife.

The shore, stretching for two miles west from Portwrinkle as far as The Long Stone headland, is a Site of Special Scientific Interest (SSSI), named for the Eglarooze Cliffs. A dense scrub of blackthorn, gorse and bracken dominates, with thrift and sea campion in the more open patches. Scientifically, the cliffs are important for the occurrence of a number of unusual or declining species of plants and butterflies, including two plants that are in the British Red Data Book of rare and endangered species: the slender bird's-foot trefoil and carrot broomrape. The Long

Low tide, luminous seaweed and boats inside the reef at Downderry

Beaches: Downderry, looking east towards Rame Head (left); Seaton (right)

Stone and, further offshore, The Brawn are often covered with hundreds of seabirds.

The coastal footpath passes the ruins of St Germans Hut, originally built as a hunting lodge for the Earl of St Germans, and zigzags down the cliff towards Downderry.

The original village of farmers' and fishermen's cottages developed on an almost flat shelf of land just a few metres above a sandy, extensive beach – an unusual site for southern Cornwall. The soils could be easily farmed, supplemented with sand and seaweed readily available on the beach. There is no harbour, but a natural reef protects a few small boats that traditionally caught lobsters and crabs as well as mackerel with handlines.

That same reef could also be a hazard for sailing ships blown on to the shore by a southerly gale. In 1901, the tea-clipper *Gypsy*, a sister ship for the *Cutty Sark*, was wrecked here. Some of its timbers found their way into local houses as lintels and doorframes, and scuba divers explore what remains on the seabed.

The modern village feels quiet and comfortably complete, with little sign of its historic roots. Its south-facing position above the beach, with views east towards Rame Head and west to Looe Island, has attracted a growing population of incomers since the late-nineteenth century; St Nicholas' church opened in 1884 to serve the expanding community.

The houses are neat with well-kept gardens. A slipway leads to the beach where boats are drawn up on the sand; but these are for sport and pleasure rather than for commercial fishing. In spite of its fine restau-

rant and the inn above the beach, and perhaps because of its limited space for parking, Downderry does little to attract the crowds of day-trippers that might otherwise flock to the village. Below the footpath to the east, but not easily accessible from it, a stretch of the beach has been adopted by naturists.

To the west, the cliffs are in danger of being undercut by the sea, so a protective wall now runs for most of the way to

Seaton Valley Country Park and Nature Reserve

Downderry's near neighbour, Seaton. This, too, is a village with little sign of a history. It sits at the mouth of the Seaton River with modern houses, shops and restaurants on either side of the wide valley; between them, the road, car-park and grassy parkland are low enough to be at risk of flooding when the tide is high and after heavy rain.

The accessible sand and shingle beach is Seaton's most obvious attraction. In summer it is typically well populated with families swimming and playing on the beach. Off-season, there may be just a couple or two walking their dogs.

Behind the village, much of the lower part of the Seaton Valley has been declared a Countryside Park and Local Nature Reserve. There was once a caravan site here, but since 1995 the County has acquired

50 ha to be managed as a green space for local residents and for nature conservation. For a mile or so a level, surfaced Valley Trail, wide enough to be a cycle and jogging path, winds its way parallel to the river and past woodlands, ponds, benches and discrete signposts with notes on the local wildlife. A narrower, muddier Otter Trail leads further upstream towards the village of Hessenford.

A diverse range of habitats – wet woodlands, meadows, ponds, riverbanks and ancient semi-natural woodland on the eastern side of the valley – means a variety of wildlife may be seen throughout the year, including lichens, bryophytes, otters, kingfishers, dragonflies, damselflies and crickets. The local Friends volunteer group reports signs of dormice – good indicators of the health of the local environment. The main scientific significance of the Reserve lies in the variety of its fritillary butterflies and moths.

Hessenford lies at the bottom of the steep-sided valley, bisected by the busy main road from Plymouth. Despite the traffic, there are two reasons for visiting: the Copley Arms, a picturesque seventeenth-century coaching inn beside the road and river; and, on a steep hill above, the church. Originally built as a chapel and dedicated to St Anne in 1833, it became a parish church 20 years later when the village had a population several times what it is now. The pretty lich-gate was added in 1905. Inside is a fine carved stone pulpit and stained glass windows depicting a harp-playing King David and a studious St Paul. The churchyard extends further up the hill and must be one of the steepest in Cornwall. It provides a fine view beyond the spire and its golden weathercock, and out over the wooded sides of the valley below.

Heading west from Seaton and halfway to Millendreath, the coastal footpath passes below a quite unusual institution. The Monkey Sanctuary was founded almost 50 years ago as a co-operative enterprise to care for monkeys that have suffered in and been rescued from Britain's trade in pets. Originally dedicated to woolly monkeys, the Sanctuary has more recently taken in other varieties. It is open to the public, widely advertised and well prepared to receive visitors, but its main aims are the welfare of its monkeys and the education of school groups and the public concerning the dangers faced by primates both in captivity and in the wild, and the need for conservation measures. As a bonus, a colony of lesser horseshoe bats has established itself in the basement of the old manor house, and may be observed through specially installed cameras.

Hessenford: St Anne's church and the Copley Arms

Millendreath today is surely the saddest place in our area. It is, potentially, a beautiful little settlement within a charming, tree-lined valley above a fine sandy beach, Cornwall in microcosm. The valley was originally developed as a resort for miners from South Wales, and a concrete, three-storey 'holiday complex' was built on the edge of the beach including cafés and shops, with rows of flats on the western side of the valley. In the 1960s and 1970s, Millendreath became a favourite holiday destination for a generation of children; but those who have returned as adults have been badly disappointed.

The concrete structure beside the beach has fallen into disuse and is now derelict and a target for vandals. A square factory building nearby dominates the land immediately above the beach. The flats are still occupied, and there might be someone fishing from the quay or a few people wandering on the sand, but the place has a decayed, depressed, abandoned atmosphere. At the time of writing, a developer is proposing a wholesale redevelopment that will 'provide Looe with a first-class tourism offer'. Maybe. But for the time being many will judge Millendreath a place to hasten past rather than linger in, hoping the planners have learned important lessons from their mistakes.

The Valley of the East Looe River

Liskeard

Liskeard is the largest town in our area. It lies near the head of the East Looe valley, on a hill well above the level of the river. Two of Cornwall's main transport links pass through or by it – the A38 highway and the mainline railway. Originally a market town, Liskeard grew rapidly during the nineteenth-century boom in the nearby mining district of Caradon on the edge of Bodmin Moor to the north. The elegant buildings dating from that period are its chief modern-day attractions.

Several ancient sites may be found in the countryside within a few miles of Liskeard: the barrows of Boconnoc Down; the stone circles at Minions and Duloe; the Doniert Stone near St Cleer, and the Giant's Hedge that extends from Lerryn and Looe – which suggests that there has been some kind of settlement on the site of the present town for at least 1,500 years. Writing in the *Britannia Depicta* atlas in 1720, John Owen believed a Roman legion was based there.

The name probably derives from the old Cornish word *Lis* or *Lys*, meaning court or palace, and a personal name Cervyd or Kerwyd; over the centuries many alternative spellings have been used. The earliest-known documented reference to 'Lyscerruyt' concerned the freeing of a slave about AD 1000. The Domesday Book of 1086 lists the manor of Liscarret as one of the most valuable holdings in Cornwall. Subsequent documents refer to Lyskerret, Leskiret, Leskyrd, Leskyret and eventually, in and since 1624, Liskeard.

The castle is a mystery. It was probably built by Richard, Earl of Cornwall, in the late thirteenth or early fourteenth century, on a site that is now a park, and which still provides a fine view over the roofs of the modern town. But it seems not to have been important enough to mention in later documents that referred to other local castles at Launceston, Trematon and Restormel. When John Leland visited Liskeard in 1538, he found only a few remains, and a survey of crown lands in 1649 reported the castle as 'much ruined and in decay, the materials being not worth the taking down.'

The town of Liskeard beyond the mainline railway

In 1240, the town was granted the first of a series of eighteen charters that have provided an evolving framework for local governance. They set not only the numbers of burgesses and aldermen and how they should be appointed, and the dates when markets and fairs should be held, but also requirements for hygiene, conducting business and even attending church. The charter of 1586, for example, forbade the washing of pilchards in the street and the spreading of false gossip to discredit other people, and imposed a fine of 12 pence for failing to attend the Sunday service. These fines were 'to be employed for the use of the poorer sort,' who presumably had joined in the hymns and prayers.

Liskeard town centre: The Parade and Barras Street, with the memorial fountain

Liskeard was one of Cornwall's five original coinage towns, where tin and other metals were traded. But the period when mining provided the main basis of the local economy was relatively short. For much of its history, Liskeard has been mainly a market centre for livestock and other farm products. Its mills served the surrounding communities. Spinning wool to produce yarn for weavers in Devon, and the manufacture of related equipment, provided an important source of employment until the spread of James Hargreaves' 'spinning jenny' led to the decline of manual production towards the end of the eighteenth century.

A charter of 1201 established Foweymoor – now Bodmin Moor – as one of four Cornish stannaries, or mining districts, where a set of laws and privileges specific to workers in the mining industry was to be applied. In 1307, Liskeard was appointed as the town where all the tin brought from Foweymoor was to be traded, and the coinage, or tax on smelted tin, collected. But this was no guarantee of prosperity: in 1569, a document reported that in 'the space of sundry years now lately passed no days of coinage [were] kept at Lyskerd… [a town now] sore decayed and greatly impoverished.'

Though some distance from the coast, Liskeard was not unaffected by smuggling. Brandy and other illegally imported goods passed through on the way from Looe or Polperro to buyers upcountry, hidden from the authorities in what was often a literally underground trade. According to William Paynter's updated edition of John Allen's *History of the Borough of Liskeard*, 'It has always been believed that Liskeard is honeycombed with tunnels and cellars… and at one time a tunnel ran from the Parish Church into Dean Street, with a branch cutting up Barras Street under Stewart House and finishing at the back of Parade House, now the site of the new Post Office.'

John Wesley visited Liskeard six times between 1751 and 1789, and described it as 'one of the largest and pleasantest towns in Cornwall,' perhaps because he found a receptive audience for his sermons. He might have formed a different view if he had had a close look a few years later, as we shall see. Nevertheless, Methodism as a religious and social movement grew rapidly during and following Wesley's visits.

The mining boom of the eighteenth and nineteenth centuries, combined with improvements in communications and other changes, had an enormous impact on Liskeard and its surrounding communities. Completion of a canal from Looe to Moorswater in 1828 greatly eased the transport of bulk goods, both fertilizers coming in and metals going out. The production of tin, copper and other metals increased dramatically, before declining equally quickly from 1860 to 1900. Censuses show that Liskeard's population rose from 2,708 in 1801 to 4,700 70 years later, then fell below 4,000 in 1891 as the mines failed.

There is a dark side to the story. Outbreaks of cholera in 1832 and 1849 caused 27 deaths the first time and 15 the next. Wilkie Collins stayed a night here in 1850, disliked it, and was anxious to leave the next day. Writing in 1856, John Allen described 'frightfully crowded' rooms, of which 'fever and immorality were the natural consequences'.

Liskeard: Foresters Hall (left), and St Martin's churchyard (right)

In 1858, a London doctor, William Rendle, passed through, and wrote to *The Times* of a steadily rising death rate resulting from 'gullies full of solid filth steaming in the sun'. In two houses he found dead children, and in others children 'hopelessly ill with a putrid disease'.

The squalid living conditions were matched by the kinds of social problems that the Wesleyans railed against: drunkenness, bull- and badger-baiting, cock fighting and sometimes ruinous gambling.

But by 1900 things had improved. The mainline railway arrived in 1859, bringing much easier and quicker communication with London and the rest of the country. And there were great improvements in public health, many of them planned by the local architect Henry Rice, who also designed many of the buildings that remain prominent features of the modern town.

In 1976, the A38 was rerouted to avoid the town centre, to the great relief of the residents. But more than enough traffic still passes through Barras Street to distract from some of Liskeard's best buildings, and much of the development since the 1960s has not enhanced the place. Yet along the Heritage Trail, evidence of the twists and turns of Liskeard's history is still plain enough.

The church is dedicated to St Martin of Tours. Most of the present building dates from the fifteenth century, and it is one of the largest parish churches in Cornwall, impressive from the outside set in its large, almost park-like churchyard on the edge of the upper end of the town; and spacious inside,

Liskeard: The 1859 Guildhall, designed by Henry Rice (left); the Bookshop under the Liberal Club (right)

with a chancel, nave, north aisle, south aisle, Lady Chapel and vestry, divided by stately granite arches. Worth exploring are the ornate font and its cover; the seventeenth-century pulpit of richly carved oak; a number of windows, including one depicting St Peter raising Dorcas, or Tabitha, from the dead; and an elaborate memorial to military and civilian sacrifices during the world wars. The present tower was completed in 1903 and has four stages, enclosing a peal of eight bells that often ring out across the town.

The Pipe Well, in Well Lane, occurs where four permanent springs emerge, and is thought to mark the centre of the original settlement. Nearby the 1859 Guildhall with its prominent clock tower is one of the more elegant features of the town centre. Next door, Foresters Hall (1896) houses the tourist information office and a museum. The large, square Webb's House, formerly Webb's Hotel, was a classic early Victorian market-town hotel that has featured in Liskeard's public events for more than 100 years. It was restored and converted into flats, and is home to the local newspaper, *The Cornish Times*.

A number of fine Henry Rice buildings line The Parade and Barras Street. His work has left a lasting impression, not only in the centre but also on residential streets such as Dean Terrace and Station Road. Rice designed the memorial fountain, which was given to the town by Michael Loam, the son of the inventor of the 'man engine' – a device for lifting men up and down mineshafts which was used in many mines in Cornwall.

At the lower end of Barras Street are the library building, donated by Cornish journalist and philanthropist John Passmore Edwards, and Stuart House, used by Charles I as a lodging in 1644 and now restored as a community building for arts, heritage and community events. It is home to the Liskeard Old Cornwall Society and its extensive archives.

The Caradon Mining District

As noted above, much of Liskeard's nineteenth-century growth and prosperity came from the mines that were developed a few miles to the north, in the Caradon mining district. This is centred on the little hamlet of Minions, from which beautiful moorland views in all directions are punctuated by the stone chimneys of iconic Cornish engine houses. The remains of 59 mines protrude or hide within the area, together with dismantled bridges and railway lines, roughly hewn cart tracks, fenced-off mine shafts sunk into the granite, overgrown water courses and flooded pits from which tin has been scoured for centuries. In 2006, this was one of ten areas inscribed as Britain's twenty-fourth UNESCO World Heritage Site – officially known as the Cornwall and West Devon Mining Landscape.

Signs of the early removal of surface deposits of tin remain as undulations in the moorland, though they are difficult to separate from the far more devastating activities of the mid-nineteenth century. The discovery of large underground deposits of copper in

Caradon, Bodmin Moor: Remains of the New Phoenix mine (left); the Prince of Wales mine (right)

1836 set off a mining boom as new shafts were sunk in search of both copper and tin.

It was a remote site with poor roads and few settlements. The Liskeard and Caradon railway, linked with the canal from Looe to Moorswater, below Liskeard, had to be built on difficult gradients to bring in heavy mining equipment and to carry out the ore. The railway eventually extended around Caradon Hill, and neat lines of granite railway sleepers still follow the contours as far north as Kilmar Tor.

Thousands of miners came from the more established sites further west, and set up

Granite railway sleepers near Kilmar Tor

often lawless shanty towns that became the modern villages of Pensilva, Upton Cross and Common Moor, as well as Minions, which did not exist before 1863.

Within a few decades the boom was over. Copper extraction had peaked by the 1850s, and tin production fell steadily. The Prince of Wales shaft was the last to close, in 1914. The local population declined rapidly in the second half of the nineteenth century as workers left for newly discovered mining centres all over the world.

Nature has hidden most of the scars. Ferns, foxgloves and moorland grasses have grown over the mine tailings; reeds have filled leats, ponds and the remains of granite quarries, bringing insects, butterflies and birds – some found in few other parts of Cornwall.

The Hurlers, Minions, Bodmin Moor

The crumbling ruins of some of the engine houses have been renovated, and the abandoned railways promoted as walking trails. Houseman's 1881 engine house near Minions was restored and opened as a Heritage Centre in 1993. The views over the moors to the north and west, and over the farms of the Tamar valley to the east are as beautiful as ever. The Bronze Age Hurlers circle of granite standing stones, a few steps from Minions and a favourite with visitors and moorland ponies, survived the boom and bust.

Possibilities for walking are almost limitless – from a stroll on nearly level ground to the distinctive Cheesewring a mile to the north, to a tougher trek into the moor beyond Kilmar Tor and back to Minions for a glass in the Cheesewring Hotel or tea in Hurlers Halt.

A steam train marking the 150th anniversary of the opening of the Looe Valley Line

For more intrepid walkers, from Minions it is possible to follow footpaths and narrow lanes to the south, through Darite and St Cleer and back to Liskeard, or along what remains of the old Liskeard and Caradon railway beside the upper reaches of the East Looe River and on to Moorswater. Either way, heading south from Liskeard is best done by train.

Looe Valley Railway

The Looe Valley Line is one of the most picturesque branch railways in England. The railway opened in 1860 to provide a route to the coast for the granite and copper mines of Bodmin Moor, following the towpath of the canal that it soon superseded. Passenger services started in 1879, and in 1901 the line was extended by a steeply rising loop from Coombe Junction to the level of the main London–Penzance line at Liskeard. The man responsible for this tricky piece of engineering was Joseph Thomas, whom we will meet again in Looe.

After the steep grade down from Liskeard, the single-track railway follows the valley of the East Looe River, with glimpses through the trees of secluded farmhouses and grazing sheep and cattle, a carpet of spring and summer flowers, and wading birds on the salt marsh after the route reaches the pretty tidal estuary.

Passengers may leave and rejoin the train at any of the little stations. Visiting the nearest villages requires a stiff uphill trek out of the valley, but there are beautiful walks along the lanes parallel to the river, past cottages decked with flower baskets and between high hedges covered in summer by the invasive but pretty Himalayan balsam.

Near St Keyne station is the Magnificent Music Machines Museum, established in the old Lametton Mill in 1967, where a 1929 Wurlitzer organ is the main attraction. Readers of Daphne du Maurier's Cornish novels may recall Lametton Mill from the early life of the main character in *The King's General*.

Evening primrose and Himalayan balsam on the bank of the East Looe river

Sandplace, the train's last stop before Looe, is where 200 years ago barges dumped sand from local beaches for spreading on the fields as a fertilizer. Below Terras Bridge, the final section of the line follows the eastern shore of the estuary, where boats are moored and the town of Looe begins.

Trains on the Looe Valley Line operate throughout the year and carry local shop-

The holy well of St Keyne

pers, schoolchildren and commuters as well as visitors. Occasionally there are specials: in 2010, a steam train made several runs to celebrate the line's 150th anniversary. Or more accurately, it was a steam train with a diesel engine at the rear to cope with the steep gradient between Liskeard and Coombe.

None of the churches of the East Looe valley is easily accessible from the train; and it is wise to check that they are open before visiting. In St Keyne, the church is dedicated to the daughter of the fifth-century King Broccan, and she is supposed to have performed many miracles in the area. She established a holy well that lies beside the lane leading from the church towards the river, which is still often visited. The church itself is beside the main road, to the south and above the

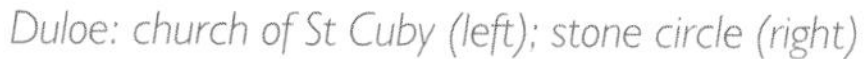

Duloe: church of St Cuby (left); stone circle (right)

village. Most of the present building dates from the fifteenth century, but a restoration in 1868 'refloored, reglazed, repewed, reroofed and wrecked' the old building, according to John Betjeman. Perhaps so, but it is now beautifully and lovingly maintained, and well worth visiting and supporting.

The church of St Cuby at Duloe was also built on an ancient holy site. The unusually squat tower with its distinctive pyramidal roof was built in the thirteenth century; a third storey added later leaned dangerously and was removed during restoration work carried out in 1861. In spring, daffodils line the pretty, well-maintained churchyard.

Nearby, at the back of an otherwise unremarkable field on the edge of Duloe is a stone circle that dates from late in the Bronze Age. This is perhaps the most significant archaeological site in our area. The eight quartz-rich, rough-hewn stones were probably carried from Herodsfoot, about two miles to the north-west. After some mid-nineteenth century restoration work they now stand, up to 2.65 m tall, in a circle of just 12 m diameter.

Part way down the road from Duloe to Sandplace is Westnorth Manor Farm, the home of Cornish Orchards, which uses over 60 varieties of traditional Cornish apples to produce award-winning blends of juice and cider. Sheep graze beneath the blossoms, and Cornish Orchards prides itself on using environmentally sensitive methods to manage its own trees and to help restore and support those on neighbouring farms. Visitors are invited to take a guided look around, when time permits, and to buy a bottle or two in the farm shop.

Cornish Orchards, Duloe (above). Ramsons in the woods above Sandplace (left)

Further on, in spring the woods lining the road are carpeted with some of the best displays of bluebells and ramsons in the area.

Morval lies on the eastern side of the valley. In a secluded lane it has an attractive church dedicated to St Wenna, with Victorian windows and carved wood in the pulpit and benches. In the south transept there is a slate

Clockwise from top left: churches of St Wenna and St Martin; East Looe river; steam fair, Morval

monument of 1637 to one of the Coode family from the nearby Morval manor. Each August the Morval Steam Fair is held near the curiously named No Man's Land, attracting beautifully restored and maintained engines from all over Cornwall and Devon.

St Martin's, the parish church of Looe, is a mile or so north of the town, nestled below the main road from Plymouth, and 'smacks of fishermen home from the sea and safe inland by a sheltered mile,' says Betjeman. The imposing Norman doorway dates from 1140, although the granite arcades and much of the interior have a fifteenth-century appearance with some early twentieth-century additions. The church is well lit at night, and makes an attractive sight for vehicles passing on the road above.

The Valley of the West Looe River

The church, St Pinnock

The West Looe River rises below the village of Dobwalls on the A38 highway. For much of their length it and its tributaries follow steep-sided, wooded valleys, passing the remains of old water mills, crossed by bridges and fords and linked by networks of narrow lanes, bridleways and footpaths – all signs of a more industrious past but well away from any busy modern routes.

The headwaters of the river lie within the old parish of St Pinnock, named for an early Welsh missionary about whom little is known. The church, with its distinctive flat, round-cornered tower, stands beside a handful of stone cottages and the former school, isolated from the parish's main settlements of East Taphouse and Trevelmond. St Pinnock is perhaps best known now for its brass band, which often plays at local events.

Herodsfoot

Four deep, tree-lined valleys come together at Herodsfoot – a name derived from the Cornish for 'at the foot of the long hill', which also serves as the title of Sally Hall's local history of the village. It is a secluded place,

Bridge over the West Looe river near Herodsfoot (above). Village green and war memorial (right)

surrounded by hills and accessible only by narrow lanes that descend steeply through the woods to a few cottages, a bridge and a small village green beside the river. This is a 'fortunate village', one of just 50 throughout the country that lost no soldiers in the two World Wars; the memorial on the green lists those who served, not those who died.

An unlikely place, then, for a mining boom; and yet that is what took place here in the mid-nineteenth century, briefly transforming Herodsfoot from what Sally Hall describes as 'a scattering of cottages and farms, well endowed with orchards', into one of Cornwall's principal sources of lead and explosives.

The presence of good-quality lead and silver in local rocks had been known for centuries, but early attempts to exploit it had never amounted to much. The first serious investment in the original North Herodsfoot Mine took place in 1844, and during the following years new and ultimately more profitable shafts were sunk to the south of the village. Some 19,000 tons of lead were sold from 1848 to 1884. Meanwhile, in 1845 a gunpowder works opened on the site of old charcoal workings in the woods to the west of Herodsfoot. Workers were drawn in from neighbouring villages and from the old mining areas of West Cornwall; the population of the village grew from barely 100 in 1841 to a peak of about 500 in the 1870s.

Soon after the boom came the bust. The main mines closed in 1884, although some small-scale copper mining continued for a few more years. The gunpowder factory closed in 1898, though later it re-opened and continued to function until 1965. The population fell steadily to the present level of 132 adults, accompanied by an all-too-familiar loss of services within the village. The school closed in 1946; the chapel in 1964, and the last shop and post office in 1993.

The gunpowder works has become the Forestry Commission's attractive Deerpark resort of cabins and woodland walks, and a few improbable engine-house chimneys can still be seen around the village. Some beautifully intricate, sparkling bournonite and tetrahedrite samples from the mines are displayed in the Royal Cornwall Museum in Truro. The main legacy of the boom years is the church.

All Saints was built in 1850 in response to the growing village population, designed by the young architect George Edmund Street who went on to build London's Royal Courts of Justice, among other prominent buildings around the country. All Saints has a distinctive shape with its steeply sloped slate roof and a bellcote above the west wall; the heavy iron door hinges are typical of Street, and the peaceful interior is well lit by the diamond-patterned stained glass windows, restored in 2006. Few churches can benefit from such a prominent position on a hill overlooking the communities they serve.

To the south of Herodsfoot a series of lanes, bridleways and footpaths follows close

All Saints church, Herodsfoot

beside the river through an almost continuous corridor of woodland, past Churchbridge, Sowden's Bridge, Watergate, the estuary and all the way to the town of Looe. If you can get a ride to Herodsfoot, this makes for an excellent, undemanding and almost traffic-free walk of five miles or so.

Pelynt

Well above the West Looe River and two miles further west is Pelynt, another village sadly divided by what has become a busy road. Yet there is a good deal of interest here,

A March morning mist, West Looe valley near Pelynt (above). Summer at St Nun's church (left)

both within the village and nearby within the parish. Not least, Pelynt can claim to be the home of one of Cornwall's principal heroes, and of the county's 'national anthem'.

Recorded as 'Plunent' in the Domesday Book, the name originally meant 'the parish of St Nun', also known as St Ninnis or St Nonna, to whom the church and other nearby antiquities are dedicated. Old cottages cluster around what is left of the village green, and the remains of three former Methodist chapels may be detected along Summer Lane – one part way up the hill, another at the top and now known as The White House, and a third hidden beside Outways farm. The Wesleyan Chapel on Jubilee Hill still functions as an important community centre, just a few steps from the pretty Jubilee Inn.

St Nun's church is thought to have been built on an old Christian site during the fifteenth century, though parts of the tower are probably older. There were later repairs and modifications, especially late in the nineteenth century when the pews and most of the windows and parts of the roof were replaced and some old monuments removed. Nevertheless, enough survives to make a visit worthwhile. The tower contains a peal of six bells dating from early in the seventeenth century that still enlivens weddings, services and important village occasions. And as usual the church embodies a great deal of local history, including some impressive monuments and plaques commemorating, among others, the Achyms, the Bullers, the Grigsons and the Trelawnys – all prominent local families.

The Achyms and Bullers were landowners. Geoffrey Grigson, born in 1905, was one of six sons of William Grigson who served as the vicar of St Nun's from 1891 to 1928. Geoffrey became a poet, prolific writer, journalist and literary critic; among many works, he wrote *The Freedom of the Parish* – an erudite reflection on country life and his profound 'sense of place', based mainly on his childhood in Pelynt.

But surely the best-known son of Pelynt was Jonathan Trelawny. Born at the nearby Trelawne Manor in 1650, he became Bishop of Bristol and in 1688 was famously tried for treason for refusing to read out a 'declaration of indulgence' that would have extended certain religious freedoms to Roman Catholics. He was acquitted on 30 June 1688 – a day of great rejoicing in Cornwall that is still celebrated in Pelynt each year. Many years later the poet and Vicar of Morwenstow, RS Hawker, wrote *The Song of the Western Men*, a poem based on Trelawny's arrest and the widespread popular demand for his release. It was set to music, and as the unofficial 'Cornish national anthem' it still inspires rugby teams and audiences at almost any performance of Cornwall's many choirs.

Beyond the village, the parish of Pelynt includes an unusual concentration of ancient archaeological sites. Nearest the village, to the south, is a collection of 'bowl barrow' remains of a Bronze Age burial ground. They

St Nonna's well, above the West Looe river (above and left). Kilminorth and Trenant woods (facing page, top); Kilminorth (facing page, bottom)

were excavated in 1830 and again in 1845, revealing among other finds a dagger that appears to have come from the Eastern Mediterranean in about 1500 BC.

In a field a mile west of Pelynt are the low circular ramparts known as Bake Rings – the remains of a settlement enclosure thought to date from late in the Iron Age or early in the Roman period. To the east and of a similar age, Hall Rings is a hill fort on a spur overlooking the West Looe valley, though much of it has disappeared into a frequently ploughed field.

Further east again, beside the lane to Hobbs Park on the steep western side of the valley, is a holy well dedicated to St Nun and marked on the OS map as St Nonna's Well. The well's stone bowl is lined with tiny, doll-like figures representing angels. Not far away and within the circle of another Iron Age hill fort there was once a chapel, also dedicated to St Nun and recorded in documents dating from 1241.

Finally, immediately below that hill fort and for a short distance built into its ramparts,

there is the Giants Hedge. This is a remarkable linear earthwork that extends for eight miles from Lerryn in the west, continuing almost to Looe. It is thought to have been built in the sixth century and to mark the northern boundary of a post-Roman kingdom, perhaps of the legendary King Mark. In places the 'hedge' is 2 m high, the same distance wide, and with a parallel ditch on its northern side. In other places it has practically disappeared. But in one form or another it can be traced along the side of the West Looe valley and through the Kilminorth Woods local nature reserve, immediately north of Looe's Millpool car-park.

For many years the area of Kilminorth Woods has been well known locally as a place for idyllic country walks. In his *History of Looe* of 1823, Thomas Bond wrote of 'a most delightful walk or ride along the banks of the Western river. Now and then you are entertained with the notes and with a view of the heron, the sea-gull, the curlew, the woodpecker, the sylvan doves; and the kingfisher, as if to shew its beautiful plumage, frequently flits from the rock below, and skims along before you.'

Not much has changed, except that we could add the little egret to Bond's list of common bird species, bright white and strutting along the shore in the mud at the edge of the estuary. A boatyard built for the Second World War closed 20 years ago, and its few remains have merged into the natural landscape. Footpaths criss-cross the woods on the steep side of the valley, marked with information posts similar to those in the Seaton Valley. To a practised eye there are deer tracks; near the top of the hillside are earthen mounds of badger setts that could be a century old; and beyond is a curious oval field bounded by a stone wall, known locally as 'The Warren' but a mystery to historians. The volunteer Friends of Kilminorth Woods promote interest in and care of the woods. They recently found a dormouse in one of the tubes set up for the purpose, which, as in the Seaton Valley, is a good indicator of ecological wellbeing.

East and West Looe

The first impression of Looe is of rows of Victorian and Edwardian houses, some converted into hotels, lining the hillsides on each side of the river, with modern shop-fronts lower down; large, prominent car-parks; an amusement arcade; boats afloat moored

A traditional fishing lugger passes down the Looe river, below the seven-arch bridge

to parallel lines of big, orange buoys or on the mud when the tide is out; and, in summer, crowds in T-shirts crossing the long, low seven-arch bridge and strolling *en masse* through the main street. Like Liskeard, this is a town where many of the remaining signs of a long and colourful past are disguised or hidden. But the evidence is there for those who search, and a little effort will be rewarded.

With so many archaeological sites in the surrounding countryside – the stone circle at Duloe, Bronze Age barrows and Iron Age forts around Pelynt, the Giant's Hedge and sites further west that we will see later – it seems certain that the human occupation of the lower Looe estuary dates from a very early period. The Domesday Book records a manor at Trenant; what is now East Looe was part of the manor of Pendryn, and the area across the river was divided between the manors of Portalla and Portbyhan, the name by which West Looe was originally known. Shutta, near the modern railway station, is thought to have been settled by the twelfth century, and for some time was home to the largest number of people living in the area. It is only from the thirteenth and fourteenth centuries that a clearer picture begins to emerge.

East and West Looe were of a similar size until the rapid developments of trading in the seventeenth century gave the eastern half an advantage because of its greater space for quays and trading. Both grew up as market towns and fishing ports, with textile and shipbuilding industries, exporting granite and importing lime to fertilize the fields. As a measure of their growing importance, they provided ships and supplies for the military adventures of Edward I and II, and 20 ships for Edward III's siege of Calais in 1346 – almost as many as came from London.

John Leland visited in 1530, and described East Looe as 'a pretty market town'. It grew steadily. In his *History of East and West Looe* (1987), John Keast tells us that by the end of the sixteenth century, Looe's fishing and trading fleet included 70 ships of greater than 60 tons displacement, with three of more than 100 tons. These were large ships: by way of comparison, the old wooden luggers we see moored to the quay displace no more than about 20 tons. By 1650 there was an established export trade in pilchards as far as the eastern Mediterranean.

As in most coastal towns of southern Cornwall, legitimate trade was supplemented by smuggling, piracy and privateering. Perhaps neither took place on the same scale as in Polperro and Fowey, but Looe did suffer from retaliation raids by French, Spanish and 'Turkish' pirates similar to those who operated around Cawsand.

Unusually, Looe has no castle. The historian Thomas Bond, writing in 1823, reported a protective wall mounted with ten cannons behind what is now the beach, with other guns on the hill above; and a sixteenth-century sketch and the name 'Castle Street' are suggestive. But no evidence remains of any fortifications.

Looe was not much affected by the military campaigns of the English Civil War, but the Napoleonic Wars 150 years later disrupted both trading and fishing, and brought great hardship. A visitor in 1808 described West Looe as 'a small and miserable town and despoiled of its trade by war, exhibiting little

Competitors in the Looe lugger regatta

else at present than poverty and discontent.' However, by then two quite separate seeds of future prosperity had already been sown.

Minerals from the Caradon area were being carried down and exported in the eighteenth century and, as we have seen, the nineteenth-century mining boom led to the construction of the canal and railway and a rapid growth in the quays and port facilities of East Looe. There was a time when half the world's copper passed through the port.

More surprisingly, the town's potential as a place of recreation and leisure was recognized as early as 1800, when the first bathing machine was set up on the beach. This was a small, enclosed carriage that could be pulled

The centre of Looe and the Guildhall (left). Ye Olde Salutation Inne, East Looe (above)

to the shoreline to provide privacy as people changed their clothes and launched themselves into the waves. The first one seems not to have been used much, but was an early glimpse of Looe's post-industrial future.

Of all this, what can we still see? The first stone bridge, built in 1436, is long gone, although J.M.W. Turner's sketch *East and West Looe* in 1811 shows that it was narrow by modern standards, with fifteen arches. Plaques on each side of the river mark where it was. The present bridge was built about 100 m upstream in 1853, and widened in the 1960s to cope with the traffic.

Immediately below the bridge on the eastern bank is Buller quay, built in 1856 to store copper from Caradon. Beside it are some of the oldest and proudest wooden boats still in the harbour. *Our Daddy*, built in traditional style in 1921, is a regular participant in the town's two-yearly regatta when luggers visit from other Cornish ports and as far away as France to parade and race sedately around Looe Bay.

The 'new' guildhall with its iconic clock tower dates from 1877, and has interesting stained glass windows in the upper chamber.

Fishermen's cottages, East Looe

Further along Fore Street is the distinctive Golden Guinea restaurant, built in 1632. It was the home of historian Thomas Bond, and when he died his heir found a pot of 10,000 golden guineas hidden in a wall.

Ye Olde Salutation Inne, or 'The Old Sal', dates from the seventeenth century with an eighteenth-century façade, partly built from old ships' timbers, and with a sloping floor supposedly to let occasional floods from very high tides drain out.

Behind the beach are six parallel, narrow streets lined with cottages, perhaps originally a planned layout but with a refreshingly wide range of house shapes and styles. 'No marti-net of an architect has been here to drill the

The Old Guildhall, in the oldest part of Looe

old stone houses into regimental regularity,' wrote Wilkie Collins approvingly in 1850. 'No house has fewer than two doors leading into two different lanes; some have three, opening at once into a court, a street, and a wharf, all at different points of the compass.' Then and now.

Among them are the sixteenth-century Church House and what remains of St Mary's church, originally dedicated as a chapel of ease in 1259, though the present building is about 100 years old. It has been converted to flats, but the tower and stained glass windows are still there.

For many, the Old Guildhall is the main attraction of the oldest part of Looe. Originally built about 1500, the second storey was added in 1587 and it still has its gabled porch, outer stairway and pillory. Once a court and a jail, it is now a well-stocked and well-documented museum and the home of the Looe Old Cornwall Society.

A few steps away on the quay is a newly erected stone memorial to local engineer Joseph Thomas. After an international career, he returned to his home town towards the end of the nineteenth century, and designed and built several important structures that shaped the future of Looe. The memorial is opposite one of his best-known works on the far bank, the road to Hannafore, which passes over several stone arches around the steeply sloping cliff.

At the southern tip of East Looe is one of its most distinctive and most photographed features, the Banjo Pier, and here too we see the hand of Joseph Thomas. He designed the pier's round end in 1896, and it solved a problem of siltation in the river.

Returning to the bridge, upstream we can see the Old Mill which, for its power, made use of the rise and fall of the tide into and out of a 5-ha millpool enclosed within the West Looe estuary. Its four undershot wheels, where bricked-up archways can still be seen, operated until 1910 to grind grain for flour and bone for fertilizer. Most of the millpool has been filled in to make a car-park.

The Jolly Sailor, West Looe

Except for the 'little seaman's chapel of St Nicholas, venerable outside but Victorian within,' John Betjeman dismissed West Looe as 'purely a tourist attraction and a place of gift shops and cafés which shut as soon as the season is over.' This seems harsh, and many would judge this as the more picturesque, less spoiled side of town. The Jolly Sailor inn has survived since the fifteenth century; the

Father and son on the Banjo Pier, East Looe

hexagonal meat market, dating from 1853, remains an attractive building, and is now a flower shop; charming old cottages line much of the steep climb up West Looe Hill.

And even with its Victorian and, in places, more modern interior, the fourteenth-century St Nicholas's church retains a welcoming openness and charm. For some time it served as a guildhall and as a school; it has been extensively restored more than once. The wood of the pulpit and bench ends, and the font cover, were carved as recently as 1960. The church was originally built as a chapel of ease for the parish church at Talland, so that parishioners could avoid what was then a precarious cliff-top journey in the direction that we will shortly take.

The Coast from Looe to Lantic Bay

Looking towards Looe Island from Port Nadler

There is a story that, before Joseph Thomas built the road to Hannafore, a woman riding a horse on the old track in a storm was blown off the path and over the cliff. There are no such dangers now, and we can enjoy a stroll on the sea wall looking out to Looe Island.

The island – variously known in the past as St George's, St Michael's and St Nicho-

Looking west from Looe Island

las's – is about a mile around, 46 m high and half a mile offshore. It might have been joined to the mainland by a causeway 1,000 years ago, and it is still possible to walk out to it at the lowest spring tides each year. Like many small islands it has a special place in local folklore: Mike Dunn's *The Looe Island Story* (2005) provides an excellent account of its fascinating history.

There are those who believe that Joseph of Arimathea visited 2,000 years ago as part of his tin-trading activities, supposedly bringing his young nephew Jesus with him. The idea is based on highly speculative claims by the reverends Dobson and Lewis, who in the 1930s and 1940s collected 'evidence' of such a visit, mainly in the form of 'oral history' from various parts of Cornwall and Somerset. Few are convinced, although some 2,000-year-old artefacts found in the area suggest that there was indeed trade between Cornwall and the Eastern Mediterranean at that time.

We are on firmer ground for events since the eleventh century. Near the highest point of the island are the remains of a chapel built in 1085. Together with its twin at Lammana on the mainland opposite, the chapel was owned and controlled by the Benedictine Abbey of Glastonbury until they fell into disuse in the sixteenth century.

Since then various people, some with a shady past, are thought to have lived, farmed and fished on the island. In the eighteenth century it was a haven for smugglers. Several ships have been wrecked on the surrounding reefs; one is thought to have brought a plague of rats for which, after several failed attempts, the people of Looe devised a solution described by Wilkie Collins in 1850:

All the available inhabitants of the town were called to join in a great hunt. The rats were caught by every conceivable artifice; and, once taken, were instantly and ferociously smothered in onion; the corpses were then... eaten with vindictive relish by the people of Looe. Never was any invention for destroying rats so complete and so successful as this!

Port Nadler Bay (above). Looking across the Bay towards Hannafore (left)

The Trelawney family owned the island for 200 years. In 1940 it was bombed by the German air force, apparently in the belief that it was a warship. In 1964 the sisters Evelyn and Barbara Atkins bought the island, and Evelyn wrote two popular books describing the experience of living there. She died in 1997, and when Babs died seven years later she bequeathed the island to the Cornwall Wildlife Trust, which manages it as a nature reserve.

Looe Island is now perhaps best known for the seals that often visit the rocks on the southern, seaward side. The Trust arranges boat trips from Looe to the island; and contrary to Wilkie Collins' colourful and imaginative account, rats remain a serious conservation problem.

From Hannafore the footpath rises, gradually at first and then for a while steeply enough to need 70 steps cut into the hillside. Here we enter the second stretch of Cornwall's AONB, which extends to the Fowey estuary. At the top of the steps and as far as the Hore Stone there are fine views down to the white, sandy beach that curves around Port Nadler Bay, in spring framed by the bright yellow of gorse bushes and the delicate white flowers of blackthorn. The beach is accessible only by boat or by a steeply descending footpath that ends with a long wooden staircase; it's a place for wandering and beachcombing, and as likely as not you will be completely undisturbed.

The next bay is a different story. Talland is accessible by two lanes lined by a few farmhouses, cottages and a hotel, and its two beaches and their respective cafés and car-parks are often busy in the summer. When the tide is up the beaches become narrow, unappealing arcs of shingle, occasionally covered with a thick layer of seaweed after a storm; at low tide, wide expanses of sand appear, attracting paddlers, swimmers, sea kayaks that may be rented nearby, and even surfers when a good southerly wind picks up.

Talland Bay, near Polperro

As far as anyone knows, there has been some form of religious site on the hill overlooking Talland Bay since pre-Christian times, inspired no doubt by the beauty of the view. According to some accounts, the Cornish saint Tallanus set up a hermitage here in the fifth century, and built an altar at the junction of mysterious 'ley-lines' supposedly known to earlier Celtic settlers.

True or not, there was a church here by the thirteenth century, and parts of the original structure can be identified in the present nave and its oddly separate tower. Most of the building dates from 200 years later, and it was only then that it was dedicated to St Tallanus. Inside there is much to admire, from the peaceful, calming ambiance to the wood of the bench-ends, beautifully carved 600 years ago. Outside, as Betjeman saw it, 'well-engraved slate and stone headstones climb and descend the steep churchyard in tidy ranks.'

Aside from its beautiful outlook, the grassy slope below the church has some scientific interest. In 2010 a small part of it was declared an SSSI for the rare 'many-fruited beardless moss' that occurs here. It is difficult to identify, less than spectacular, and found in only one other known location, further west on the Roseland peninsula.

Polperro

If Talland Bay was settled before the Christian era, then we may be sure that people have lived on the site of modern Polperro for at least as long, although the closest that we have to hard evidence is a hoard of Roman coins found within the village in 1955. This was an ideal place for an early settlement, albeit a small and isolated one for most of its history. A deep, steep-sided valley follows a curving course to the sea, just wide enough at the coast to build a sheltered harbour and a few rows of surrounding houses. The villagers have always earned their living from the sea, and not only from fishing.

Traditionally, the village was divided by the stream that runs through it, forming a boundary between the manors of Killigarth to the east and Raphael to the west; and between the parishes of Talland and Lansallos. By the fourteenth century there was a chapel dedicated to St Peter high above the western side of the bay; it fell into disuse long ago, and in his *History of Polperro* (1871) Jonathan Couch described the chapel as 'almost obliterated.' It gave its name to 'Chapel Cliff' and the prominent private house nearby, Mont Saint Pierre; its stones are thought to have been

Fishing boats at low tide in Polperro's outer harbour

used to build the Net Loft that stands below Peak Rock opposite the harbour entrance.

Couch was born in Polperro in 1789, and became the village doctor and a self-taught naturalist. Based on specimens provided by his fishermen neighbours, his four-volume *History of the Fishes of the British Isles* became a standard work on the subject. As a historian, Couch provides fascinating insights into the nature of social life, work and trade in the eighteenth and nineteenth centuries, both legal and, the most interesting part, illegal.

Polperro was well suited to smuggling. Remote, honeycombed with narrow lanes and hiding places, it was hard to reach and, once there, easy to evade the law. Smuggling became such a part of life that few questioned its legitimacy. 'All joined in,' says Couch:

Polperro's inner harbour (left), and 'Roman' Bridge (right)

The smith left his forge, and the husbandman left his plough; even women and children turned out to assist in the unlawful traffic, and received their share of the proceeds. That it was in any degree a dishonest pursuit perhaps never entered their minds... The gentry of the neighbourhood bought their brandy and lace; the excise and customs house officers connived in unlawful acts and profited by secret connections with the smugglers.

Ships were built in yards inside and outside the harbour, designed to be fast enough to outrun the revenue's boats, and local fishermen regularly outwitted the revenue officers.

Many transactions originated in the Channel Islands, facilitated and financed by the local banker Zephaniah Job, another larger-than-life character from the village's past. There are numerous tales of adventure, danger, capture and escape, from the English Channel to Ireland and the Caribbean, and involving people whose descendants still live in the village.

As in Cawsand, Portwrinkle and Looe, smuggling had largely died out by 1850, not least because of the coming of the coastguard. Polperro was one of the first villages in the country where revenue officers were stationed. Their row of houses may still be seen on Talland Hill high above the harbour.

The picturesque quality of the village and of the old cottages within it – rounded, square, with an inside or outside stairway, joined up or separate, tall or just one storey high, supported by ancient wooden props above the river, and no two of them alike – has attracted artists for many years. Of the best known, the earliest was Joseph Farington who visited in 1810. Herbert Edward Butler opened an art school here late in the nineteenth century, and his paintings of the village still fetch high prices at London auctions. Oskar Kokoschka stayed and worked here for a year or so after escaping from Prague in 1938. By the 1950s it was common to see a lone figure sitting at an easel on the quay or on the harbour mud when the tide was out.

But no longer, and 60 years later it is wise to plan a visit with some care. The village can be uncomfortably overcrowded on summer days when passengers from the cars and coaches of a packed car-park take to the narrow streets. And with more and more houses around the harbour and beyond being bought by wealthy outsiders as second homes or for short-term renting, there are serious concerns for the future, as in many Cornish villages.

But, for now, there is still a year-round community with a busy school, village hall and chapel. The fishing fleet works both winter and summer, though it is smaller than it was and is greatly outnumbered in the harbour by pleasure craft. Jonathan Couch's house and its near neighbour where John Wesley brought Methodism to the village in 1760 still stand – one now a private home, the other a gift shop. Reflections in the calm, dark water beneath whitewashed cottages fringed with busy Lizzies, lobelias and begonias make the harbour a delight on a bright summer evening.

Ebenezer's Gallery in The Coombes, and the Arts Foundation above the inner quay keep the artistic tradition alive, boosted by a lively annual festival in June. The excellent Heritage Museum of Smuggling and Fishing by the harbour has photographs, models of old boats, pieces of clothing and equipment, and the written memories of past residents that recreate the atmosphere of an older Polperro and an almost forgotten way of life.

Lansallos and Lantic Bay

When Polperro is at its most crowded, the footpath westward provides a welcome and beautiful escape, although the six miles to Polruan is not the easiest of walks. At first the remains of old allotments and, in summer, patches of the orange-flowered montbretia line the south-facing slopes above the cliffs, followed by a series of sometimes-demanding descents and ascents across the mouths of the valleys of little streams. One or two sandy coves are accessible below steeply descending slopes.

Aside from their scenic value, parts of these cliffs were declared one of the country's first

The coastal footpath above the cliffs east of Lansallos beach

SSSIs, in 1951. Now covering the full distance between the two villages, this SSSI is noted for its rich variety of plant species, some of which are nationally scarce, together with colonies of uncommon butterflies and birds listed in the Red Data Book of endangered species, including the Dartford warbler, peregrines, shags and fulmars.

Lansallos cove is a good place to take a rest on the beach, or a diversion. A track

Church of St Ildierna, Lansallos (left). The beach at Lantivet (above)

heads inland for a mile, leading to another fine example of Cornish religious art and architecture. Lansallos church was dedicated to St Ildierna in 1321, and has had a turbulent recent history. It was damaged by lightning in 1923 and 1975; by military aircraft in 1941, and by a hurricane in 1990. In 2005, local vandals started a fire that threatened to destroy the building. Fortunately the church's most valuable features were saved, including the magnificent bench-ends that were carved between 1490 and 1520. By 2011 the 'charming light interior with granite arcades' that John Betjeman described had been restored, and it's worth the climb up from the beach for a look.

Beyond Lansallos is the sandy, secluded little beach at Lantivet, and further west an

Dawn breaks over Lantic Bay on a summer morning

isolated coastguard hut above the cliffs where Daphne du Maurier once worked. Then, as you walk up and over the spine of Pencarrow Head, the giant amphitheatre that is Lantic Bay unfolds before you.

There might be a gale and driving rain, with the sea far below grey, threatening and specked with white-capped waves; or on a crisp morning the rising sun will gradually draw the shadows from the shoreline, while on a summer afternoon there will be boats from Polperro and Fowey anchored offshore and families enjoying the beach. Whatever the case, pause and take a long look, because this is as fine a sight as you will see in southern Cornwall.

From here it is a short walk inland to the coast road and the bus, or on to Polruan and the Fowey estuary. It is a fitting place to end our journey.

Index

Note: References in *italic* are to illustrations.